FRENCH MINOR RAILWAYS

Vol 3

PETER SMITH

COPYRIGHT 2014 PETER SMITH

ISBN –13: 978-1494956899

ISBN-10: 1494956896

CHAPTERS

CHAPTER 1 FOULAIN—NOGENT   Page 4

CHAPTER 2 CdF de l'YONNE   Page 17

CHAPTER 3 MONTELIMAR   Page 36

CHAPTER 4 VIERZON   Page 51

CHAPTER 5 PETIT ANJOU   Page 57

CHAPTER 6 CHALON—MERVANS   Page 71

CHAPTER 7 ALLEVARD LES BAINS   Page 82

This is the third selection of French minor railway and this time they are all metre gauge simply because they are lines that I find most appealing. They range from little independent tramways serving a local community for a few years and then quietly disappearing to sections of large networks that nevertheless were no better equipped to cope with the challenges of the 1930's.

I hope you enjoy the lines I have chosen; they are varied and attractive, all typically French yet all different and distinctive.

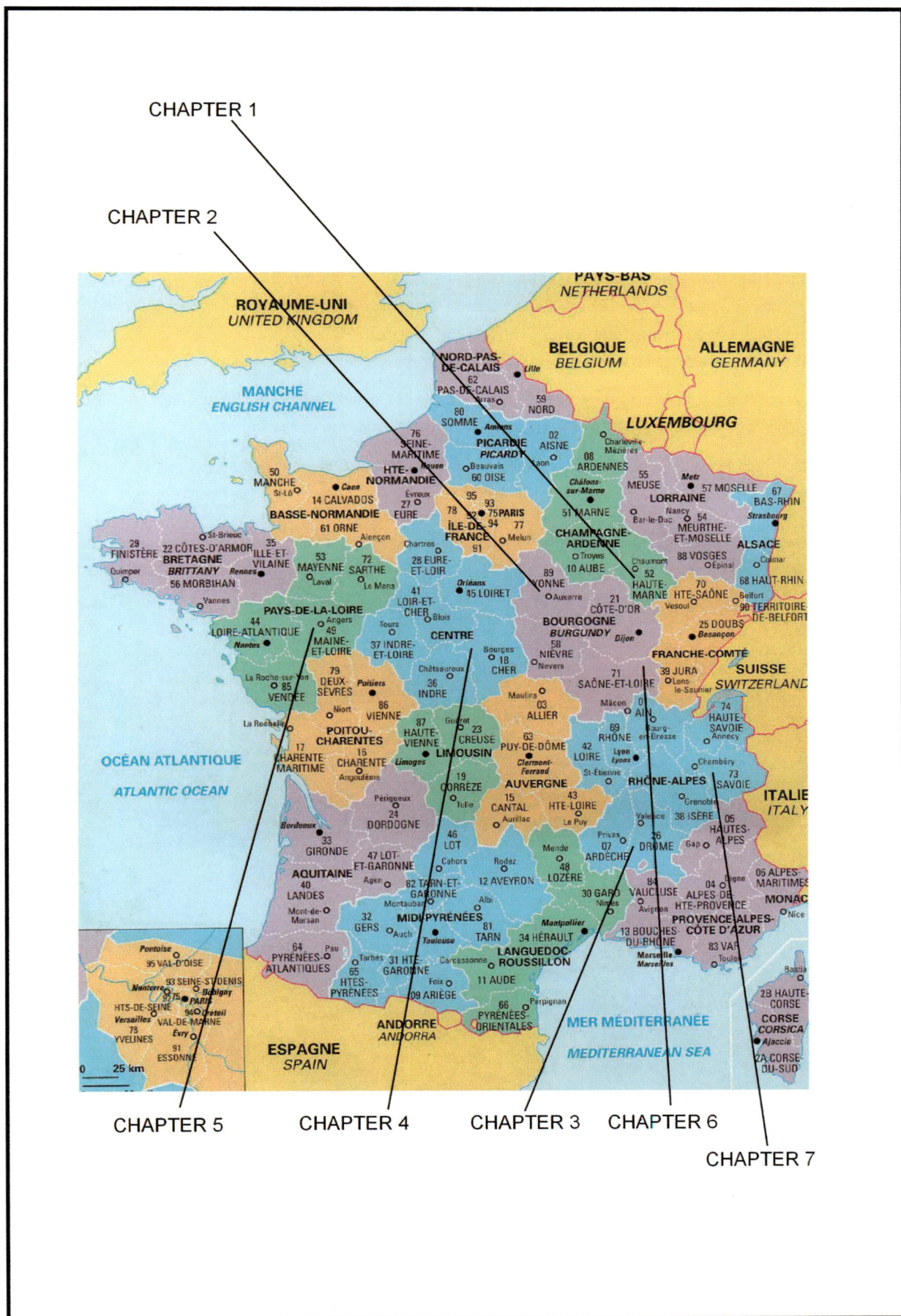

CHAPTER 1

THE FOULAIN TO NOGENT EN BASSIGNY TRAMWAY.

This is another of those little independent tramways that came to life, served their community without any fuss for a few years and then quietly faded away, largely forgotten now even in the communities they served.

Foulain was a station in Haute-Marne on the Paris East to Mulhouse main line of the Est Railway, a major trunk route opened between 1848 and 1858 though Foulain contributed few of the profits of the Est company. It was a typical small station serving a small town, where most trains ran straight through.

The tramway came into being because in Nogent en Bassigny, 12km away, there were factories with a particular speciality, cutlery and scissors; these needs an efficient outlet for their produce so the tramway company was formed in order to connect the town to the outside world. The line opened in 1904, running alongside the Est line for a short distance until it reach Foulain station. The only intermediate stop was at Poulagny.

The tramway was metre gauge and was operated with a couple of Corpet Louvet tank loco's lettered 'CFN' on the buffer beams. The loco sheds were at Nogent, and tracks went into at least one of the factories.

The tramway did well to last as long as it did; closure did not come until 1947.

I hope this pictures will give a flavour of the line, in many ways so typical of these tiny independent companies that flourished briefly all over France.

Most of the facilities at the terminus are included in this picture; the locomotive shed is on the right, with three roads so one was perhaps used for repairs. The small goods shed is attached to the station building, as typically French as you could imagine. Anyone looking for a narrow gauge terminus to model could do a lot worse than this.

Not long after the line opened Corpet Louvet no. 1 stands at the station while the crew pose for they camera. The goods shed is wooden, and the short loading bank alongside must have been sufficient to cater for local needs.

The coaches are four wheeled and two are enough to cope with the likely number of passengers. Mixed trains would have been the rule on a line such as this.

This is not such a clear picture but it does show a different train, in this case with a loaded open wagon behind the loco. It is quite possible that the company only ever owned two coaches.

It's amazing how every photographer (or the same one on different occasions) stood in just the same spot to take their pictures.

The factory looks a little out of place but in a rural area the employment it offered could be a lifeline.

The works below was served by the tramway; whether they are the same factory I don't know.

Judging by the number of grindstones this is the cutlery factory; health & safety was not a priority!

These two views show the tramway in later years, either the 1930's or 40's. still providing a valuable service.

The halt in the lower picture doesn't appear in any of the other postcards; it may have been a later attempt to attract more passengers. The two Corpet's must have been getting worn out by this time.

Back to the early days and a charming picture of Poulangy, the only intermediate station on the line. The ballast looks remarkably good; cinders and dirt were more usual on lines like this so it probably shows the line soon after opening.

Looking the other way as a train leaves the station for Foulain.

Three children have come out to have their picture taken, perhaps the family of the stationmaster.

The main line station at Foulain with a train in the platform; the tramway approached on the right from behind the photographer and terminated just out of the picture to the right of the Est platform. The line on the left is an extended siding.

In this view from a bridge the tramway is on the left and runs alongside the main line to the station. To the left of the tramway out of sight is a river which the line crossed before turning towards Nogent and away from the East main line.

Below, it looks as though the tramway is in the foreground but in fact that was a siding, the tramway was on the far side of the main line...the tramway station can be seen on the far right.

The tramway can just be seen behind the fence on the right; if you look closely a tramway train can just be made out with the station building behind it. It's a busy scene because there is also a train on the siding on the left, which may have served a works of some kind. There was no physical connection between the tramway and the Est station.

Below is a view of the Est goods yard; the caption implies a military camp which might be what was served by the long siding in front of the station building.

More military activity in the goods yard at Foulain in 1906. I haven't been able to finds any details of a siege of Langres.

More to the point, if you look to the left of the goods shed there is the tramway station building with smoke rising from a locomotive.

This is the tramway station at Foulain; the Est station footbridge is on the left. There is a small goods shed on the far end of the station building. Other than that facilities seem to have been minimal partly because it was a constricted site between the Est station and the river.

The Est station closed not long after the tramway, though I haven't been able to confirm the date; the station building is still there, hardly changed at all, as is the former Hostellerie as seen above.

CHAPTER 2

CdF DE L'YONNE   JOIGNY TO TOUCY LE HAUT.

The metre gauge system of the CdF de Yonne was quite extensive; the line I am going to illustrate was opened in 1902 and ran for 37km from outside the main line station at Joigny pretty much due south to Toucy le Haut, a branch leaving the line at Aillant sur Tholon to run to Fleury which opened at the same time.

The Yonne system used a variety of locomotives but the pictures of this line all show Pinguely or Corpet Louvet 030 tanks; the first railcar, a Renault NC type, was introduced in 1927 and ten years later Billard railcars were in use.

The stations on the line were Joingy, Chamvres, Chamvallon, Senan, Villiers sur Thonon, Aillant sur Tholon, Chassy, St Maurice sur Tholon, Egleny, Beauvoir, Parly and Toucy le Haut.

The route closed in 1938, as ever the victim of more efficient road competition.

The line began at this station in Joigny; the photographer had his back to the main line station which was on the PLM Paris to Lyon line opened in 1849. The PLM station remains open with the original building though it has been altered considerably.

Le Tacot en Gare de JOIGNY
Collection J. D., Sens

I have only been able to find three pictures of the station but they should at least give an impression of how it looked. The loco in the top pictures is Pinguely 030 tank No. 6.

73 – JOIGNY – Vue prise du « Tacot »

29 - JOIGNY — La Gare

59 - JOIGNY — Gare du P.-L.-M. (côté intérieur)

Chamvres station with Pinguley 030 No. 5 on a mixed train which has a four wheeled and a bogie coach.

The next station was Champvallon; all these little wayside stations had the same arrangement of a passing loop and a goods shed attached to the station house, with a loading platform in front of it. The end wall of the goods shed was wooden, perhaps to allow for later enlargement.

Senan was the next station, offering a useful view of the road side of the buildings.

Things look a lot bleaker on the lower picture!

At Villiers the goods shed looks to be rendered like the house; this is the view from the road with track beyond the building where the wagons are standing.

These stations certainly left you in no doubt about where you were!

Pinguley No. 4 smokes as it draws to a halt in the station to pick up four passengers.

The next station was the junction of Aillant sur Tholon where a branch left the line to connect with Fleury. There were slightly more facilities here; the water tower of course, and the station house is larger with three windows upstairs.

The gantry crane looks as though it straddled the main line which would be unusual to say the least and I think it must be alongside and over a siding or the loop line. It must have been required to lift something very heavy; blocks of stone perhaps.

The physical junction between the lines seems to have been away from the station itself.

AILLANT-SUR-THOLON. — ARRIVÉE D'UN TRAIN EN GARE

The road side of the station building; the increased length makes a more attractive structure to my eye.

AILLANT-SUR-THOLON (Yonne). — La Gare.

Everything looks brand new in this view; is that the new station master and his wife on their first day at work?

The train in the lower picture has a Corpet Louvet loco rather than a Pinguely as seen up to now, No. 24.

The next station after the junction was Chassy, as seen here it returned to the simple arrangement of a loop with small station building and goods shed attached. The point in the lower picture has rail chairs alongside the blades.

The next station was Egleny again following the same pattern and seen here soon after opening.

The station house survives here.

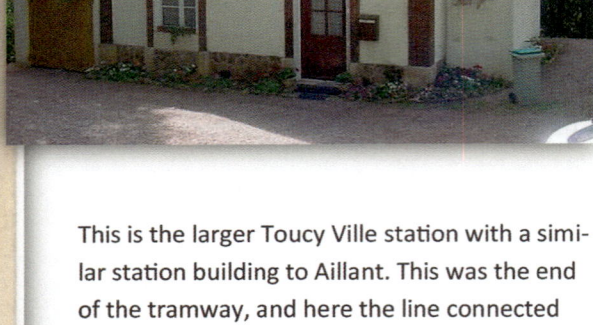

This is the last town, Toucy, where the house also survives at the former Toucy le Haut station. There is no loop or goods shed here, just a single line passing the house.

This is the larger Toucy Ville station with a similar station building to Aillant. This was the end of the tramway, and here the line connected with the PLM which also had a second station in the town making four in all! To put this into perspective, the population was around 2500.

This station building has also survived as part of a preserved line (see the next page).

There were two standard gauge lines serving the town, both PLM; one was between Auxerre and Gier and the other between Trigueres and Clamency. This is the fourth station, Toucy Moulins. Both the lines lost their passenger services in 1938, meaning that during that year the town went from having four stations to having none. However, the freight trains continued to run and now a small preservation group is established between Charmy and St Forgeau which passes through Toucy and runs a Picasso railcar.

Three views of Toucy Ville station, the last showing the preserved railcars now operated on the line.

I have not been able to establish exactly where the tramway terminated, but presumably there was a cross platform interchange of some sort.

Two views of Corpet Louvet No.22 on the Yonne system. The spark arrester on the chimney and the additional plating on the cab opening are later additions.

Of course we modellers always go to great lengths to get our buffers dead level, don't we!

CHAPTER 3

THE MONTELIMAR TO DIEULEFIT TRAMWAY

This is another small independent tramway in the Drome region, which ran from the main line station at Montelimar to the town of Dieulefit and was known as 'le Picodon'.

Dieulefit was an industrial town which badly needed a rail link in order to bring in materials and take out the finished products from the factories. The first proposal was as early as 1866, the main line through Montelimar having opened in 1854, but work did not begin on the tramway until 1892. The tramway opened in 1893; there were seven stations and a further eight halts on the route. To begin with there were two return trains a day, with a third added in 1894 and a fourth in 1904...extra trains were run on public holidays. The speed limit was 25kph, though 17kph was generally the actual average speed of the trains which was still faster than walking.

Passenger traffic was light; in 1900 the station at Begude only issued 17 tickets a day spread across three trains, and that was one of the larger places en route. Freight traffic was heavier, carrying wheat, timber, stones, sugar beet and pottery outwards and coal, wool salt and sugar inwards among other things. The company employed twenty six people.

As was so often the case World War One had a detrimental effect on the line and following the war it was no longer profitable. It closed in 1934 and the road was widened along the route to allow for greater motor traffic.

The tramway used at least one Corpet Louvet 030 tank loco and one Pinguely 030.

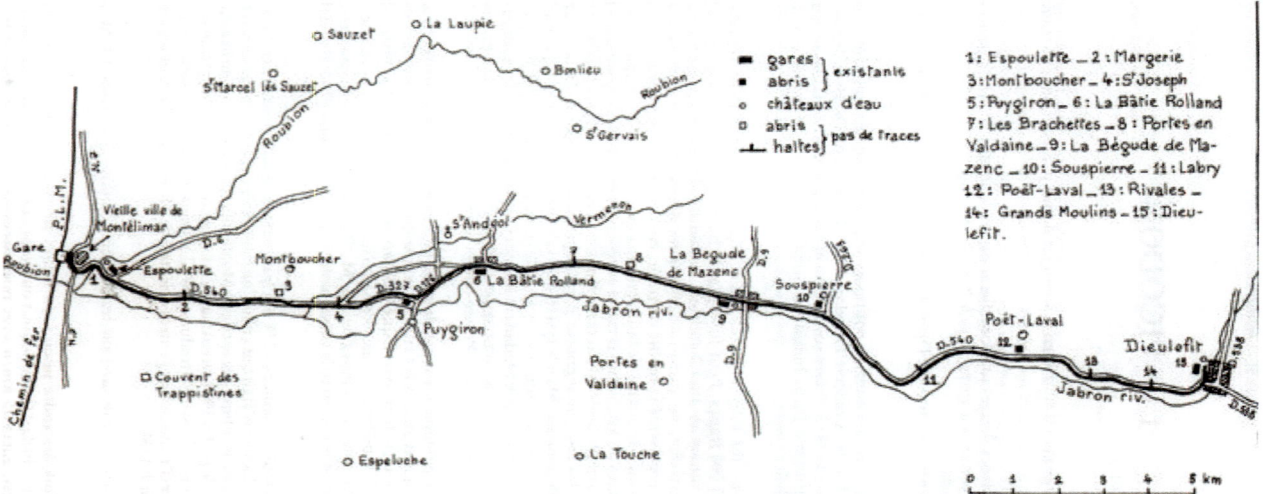

The left hand bridge carried the tramway over the river intro Montelimar.

The terminus station at Dieulefit with a train ready to leave. The goods shed is beyond the station building and the loco sheds were beyond that at the far end of the line. Leaving the station the line ran straight onto the road and then through 'Les Promenades', a public park. The station building is still there today, nicely restored.

DIEULEFIT — La Gare

Two loco's in the station, a Pinguley 030 on the left and a Corpet Louvet on the right backing onto the train.

DIEULEFIT — La Gare

A mixed train leaving the station for Montelimar behind the Corpet Louvet tank.

The trains ran alongside the road through this attractive wooded area; this is the Corpet Louvet tank on a mixed train. The coach appears to have boards along the top of the sides in the manner of an urban tramway.

Postcard: Cl. E. Girard, édit. Serre — DIEULEFIT PITTORESQUE — Les Promenades

The little 020 steam tram engine on the right is a mystery; it is lettered 'CD' and appears to be a self contained passenger carrying vehicle. It may have simply been used in the Promenades and have had no connection with the tramway proper.

Postcard: DIEULEFIT — Les Promenades

The station at Poet Laval which was pretty much in the middle of nowhere. The Copret Louvet tank appears to be numbered 15 on the buffer beam but the tramway would not have had that many loco's.

The next station was Souspierre of which no pictures have been found, and then came the larger town of Begude de Mazenc where the line ran right through the middle along the main street.

LA BéGUDE-de-MAZENC (Drôme) — La Poste et Avenue de la Gare

LA BÉGUDE-de-MAZENC (Drôme). — La Gare des C. F. D.

Although this is a much bigger place the station building is still the small brick shelter seen elsewhere. The Pinguely tank is seen on more detail.

BÉGUDE DE MAZENC (Drome) - Arrivée de la Route de Montélimar

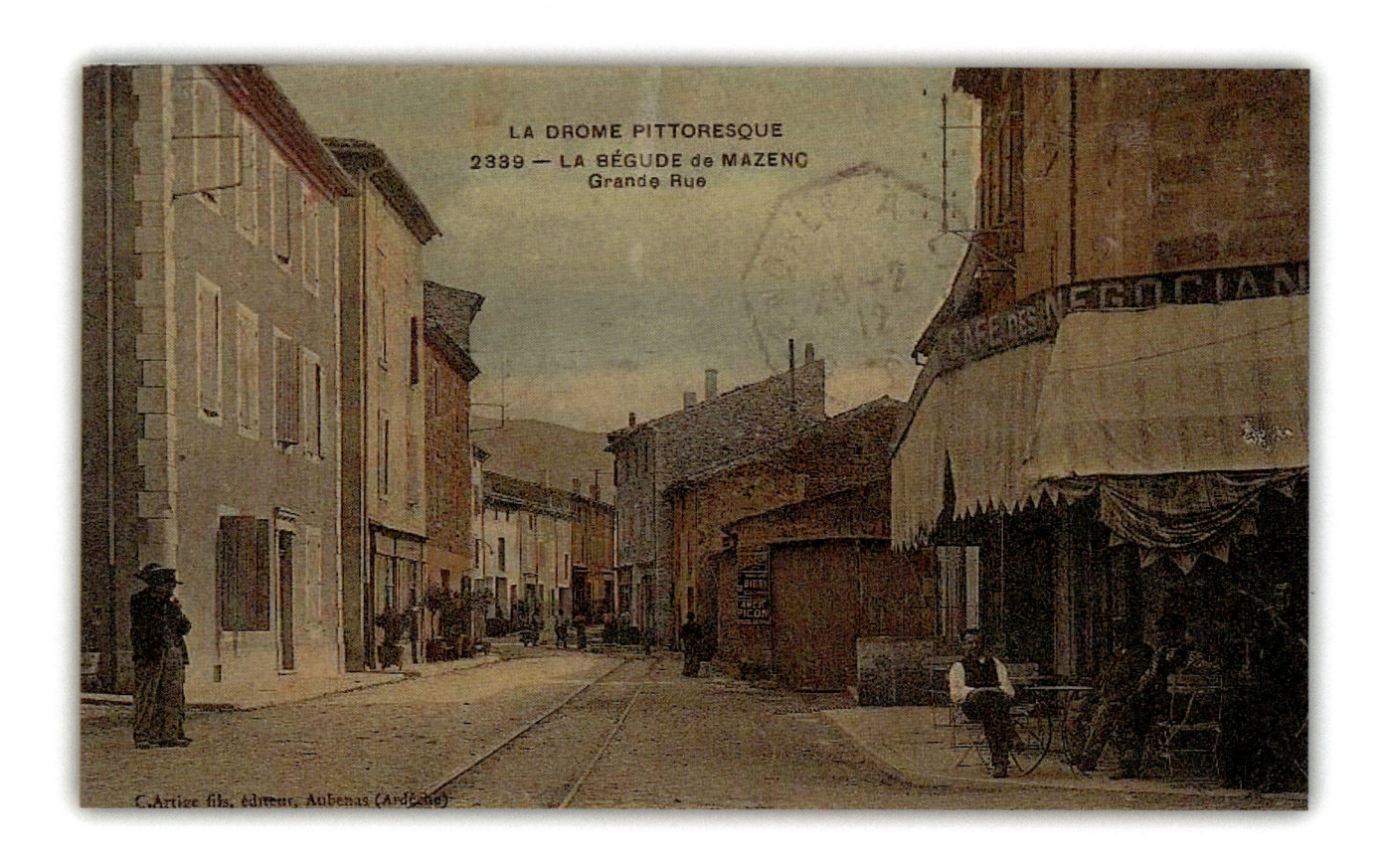

LA DROME PITTORESQUE
2339 – LA BÉGUDE de MAZENC
Grande Rue

LA BÉGUDE DE MAZENC — L'Avenue de la Gare

23 LA BEGUDE DE MAZENC – La Gare
Editions J. Brun et Cie Carpentras

It's a shame this picture isn't clearer; there's a lot of activity with the row of carts. The station building is the small building on the left.

Below is the next station, La Batie Rolland, and we can finally see that the Pinguley loco was No. 1.

LA BATIE-ROLLAND – La Gare

C. M Bouffier, édit.

The station was just a wayside halt with a passing loop, but there was at least some habitation here.

LA BATIE ROLLAND (Drôme) — La Route et le Tramway.

The postcard below is labelled 'Escoulette' which was the station before Montelimar but I have my doubts; it looks to me like the terminus at Dieulefit with the loco shed on the left. The through stations only had small single story station buildings and there would be no need to an engine shed at this location. As it is the only picture I have found unfortunately there is nothing to compare it with.

**34. MONTÉLIMAR — Gare d'Espoulette
Ligne de Dieulefit (C. D)**

6. - Montélimar. — Ses Ponts sur le Roubion et le Faubourg d'Espoulette

Two more views of the much photographed bridges over the River Roubion between Espoulette and Montelimar.

The tramway crossed the one on the left.

31 MONTÉLIMAR. — Pont Eiffel, Pont du Tramway et Quartier Espoulette. - LL

The tramway terminated outside the main line station at Montelimar, seemingly in a simple passing loop without a station building though there may have been a small shelter.

The main line station was on the PLM Paris to Lyon route and opened in 1854; it is still open and has the original station building in superb condition.

LA DROME ILLUSTRÉE MONTÉLIMAR — 13. La Gare, vue extérieure

LA DROME PITTORESQUE
2371 — MONTÉLIMAR - La Gare (Intérieur)

A tramway train can be seen to the right of the lamp post, the only picture of one in Montelimar that I have found.

The SNCF really do look after their stations; the building at Montelimar is in excellent condition with just the modern canopy looking different from the old postcards.

CHAPTER 4

VIERZON

A slightly different approach for this chapter; a large town rather than rural quaintness and an urban backdrop for a metre gauge line which is so full of character it cries out to be modelled.

The line was part of the Tramways d'Indre, and Vierzon is a town in the Cher department of the Centre region of France; indeed, the River Cher runs through the town.

The tramway opened in 1904, part of the line from Issouden via Vatan which terminated outside the main station in Vierzon. The section as far as Vatan closed in 1937, from Vatan to Vierzon in 1939. It was operated with a fleet of Pinguley 030 locomotives, rather oddly numbered 1 to 12 for the 17 ton type 107 engines, and then 50 to 53 for the four larger 20 ton type 117's.

There were three tramway stations in Vierzon, Vierzon Bourgneuf, Vierzon Ville and finally the mainline station. This had been opened as early as 1847 by the Paris Orleans Railway . Unfortunately the town and station were very badly damaged during an allied bombardment in 1944 and the present station is pretty much entirely post war.

The postcards take us back to a happier time when the metre gauge trains of the TI ran through the streets of the town and scenes like these were commonplace:

67 - Vierzon - Rue de la République - Arrêt du Tramway

Anyone looking for an urban backdrop for a layout could do a lot worse than the distinctive Merlin factory on the Rue Replublique—it appears in may of the pictures because the tramway trains stopped right outside.

The outside framed Fourgon is interesting.

Below is the other amazing building forming the backdrop to the little trains.

Cher — 50 - VIERZON, la " Société Française ", Arrêt du Tramway

The Merlin factory made agricultural machinery and may well have made use of the tramway themselves.

The French Society of Vierzon or SFMAI (French Society of Agricultural and Industrial equipment) was a company created in 1847 by Gerard Célestin in Vierzon, the French pioneer of agricultural machinery, and the building with the glass end wall is their works. The company was bought out by CASE in 1960.

Whether these two works were connected or were competitors I don't know.

2 - VIERZON (Cher) — Place de la Gare

559 — Vierzon - Place de la Gare

If you are going to build an engineering works that's the way to do it. What a fantastic building!

Vierzon — Place de la République et le Jardin Public

66 - Vierzon - Place de la Gare - Tramway de l'Indre

The Hotel de Bourdeaux extends on both sides of the works entrance. It seems odd having the hotel next to the works, but on both sides…...odder still. I wonder if this was an exhibition hall for the firm's products rather than the factory itself?

Below, a train running over the river bridge to get to the main line station where the line terminated.

Vierzon — Rue du Pont

64. VIERZON. — Pl...

COMPAGNIE DES TRAMWAYS DE L'INDRE
(1re et 2e classes.)

CHATEAUROUX A VALENÇAY

fr. c.	fr. c.	kil.	(76, 90)								
De Châteaur.			●Châteauroux...	6 20	12 40	17 10	●Valençay...dép.	6 »	10 10	16 50	
» 20	» 15	3	Déols (halte).....	6 33	12 53	17 23	Hermitage (halte)	6 13	10 23	17 3	
» 90	» 65	10	Villers...........	7 2	13 22	17 52	Vic-sur-Nahon...	6 31	10 41	17 21	
1 25	» 95	14	Vineuil..........	7 13	13 33	18 3	Langé............	6 44	10 54	17 34	
2 »	1 55	23	Levroux..........	7 49	14 9	18 39	Entraigues.......	6 52	11 2	17 42	
2 55	1 95	29	Moulins..........	8 4	14 24	18 54	Moulins..........	7 13	11 23	18 3	
3 15	2 40	36	Entraigues.......	8 25	14 45	19 15	Levroux..........	7 39	11 48	18 29	
3 35	2 55	38	Langé............	8 33	14 53	19 23	Vineuil..........	8 6	12 15	18 56	
3 70	2 80	42	Vicq-sur-Nahon..	8 46	15 6	19 36	Villers...........	8 16	12 25	19 6	
4 20	3 20	48	Hermitage (halte)..	9 3	15 23	19 53	Déols (halte).....	8 43	12 53	19 33	
4 40	3 35	50	●Valençay (79) arr.	9 15	15 35	20 5	●Châteauroux...	8 55	13 5	19 45	

ARGENTON (P.-O.) AU BLANC

fr. c.	fr. c.	kil.	(78, 80, 90)									
D'Argenton			●Argenton(P.O.)dép.		7 5	13 5	18 5	●Le Blanc (Or.)dép.	6 »	11 50	17 10	
» 25	» 20	3	Argenton-Baignett.		7 18	13 18	18 18	Villiers..........	6 30	12 20	17 40	
» 80	» 60	9	Le Puy-de-l'Age..	Mercredis et samedis.	7 45	13 45	18 45	Mauvières........	6 38	12 28	17 48	
1 30	1 »	15	Ablous...........		8 4	14 4	19 4	Bélâbre..........	7 3	12 53	18 13	
1 50	1 15	17	St-Gilles.........		8 14	14 13	19 13	Chalais...........	7 24	13 14	18 34	
2 »	1 55	23	St-Benoit-du-arr. Sault (148).. dép.		8 27 8 42	14 27 14 42	19 27 19 37	La Rochechevreux. Prissac...........	7 34 7 48	13 24 13 38	18 44 18 58	
2 45	1 90	28	Sacierges........	5 42	8 58	14 58	19 53	Sacierges........	8 3	13 58	19 18	
3 »	2 30	34	Prissac..........	5 58	9 19	15 19	20 14	St-Benoit-du-arr. Sault.........dép.	8 23 8 33	14 13 14 34	19 33 19 49	
3 40	2 60	39	La Rochechevreux.	6 19	9 32	15 32	20 27	St-Gilles.........	8 48	14 43	19 58	
3 75	2 90	43	Chalais...........	6 32	9 45	15 45	20 40	Ablous...........	8 58	14 53	20 8	
4 30	3 30	49	Bélâbre..........	6 45	Excepté les mercredis et samedis.							
					7 5	16 5	21 »	Le Puy-de-l'Age..	9 16	15 11	20 26	
4 75	3 60	54	Mauvières........	7 10	7 28	16 5	21 »	Argenton-Baignett.	9 47	15 42	20 57	
4 90	3 75	56	Villiers..........	7 28	10 28	16 28	21 23					
5 60	4 30	64	●Le Blanc (Or.)arr. (74, 78, 79, 82)	7 36 8 5	10 36 11 »	16 36 17 5	21 31 22 »	●Argenton (P.O.)	9 55	15 50	21 5	

SAINT-BENOIT-DU-SAULT A CHAILLAC

fr. c.	fr. c.	kil.	(148)					(a)	(b)	
De St-Benoit			●St-Benoit-d-Sault	8 47	14 47	19 47	Chaillac.......dép.	5 5	7 45	13 35	18 45
1 05	» 80	12	Chaillac........arr.	9 17	15 17	20 17	●St-Benoit-d-Sault	5 35	8 15	14 5	19 15

(a) Mercredis et samedis. — (b) Mercredis et samedis exceptés.

ISSOUDUN A VIERZON

fr. c.	fr. c.	kil.	(90, 109)									
D'Issoudun			●Issoudun (P.O.)..	...	7 15	13 15	18 35	●Vierzon (P.O.)dép.	3 35	7 55	14 35	19 15
» 25	» 20	3	Place de Vouet (h.)		7 22	13 22	18 42	Vierzon-Bourgneuf	3 47	8 9	14 49	19 29
» 45	» 35	5	Les Bordes........		7 39	13 41	19 1	Port-des-St-Hil. (h.)	3 56	8 19	14 59	19 39
1 15	» 85	13	Paudy............		8 1	14 8	19 24	Massay...........	4 14	8 37	15 17	19 57
1 50	1 15	17	Giroux-Villeneuve.		8 12	14 19	19 35	Provenchères (h.)..	4 23	8 46	15 26	20 6
1 65	1 25	19	Luçay-le-Libre (h.)		8 18	14 21	19 41	Nohant-en-Graçay.	4 38	9 1	15 41	20 22
1 95	1 45	22	Meunet-sr-Vatan(h)		8 26	14 29	19 49	Vilaine-Coulon (h.)	4 45	9 8	15 49	20 29
2 30	1 75	26	Vatan.......arr. dép.	5 33	8 37 8 49	14 40 16 43	20 » 20 23	Graçay.......arr. dép.	4 51 4 55	9 14 9 20	15 55 16 »	20 35 20 45
2 65	2 »	30	Reboursin (halte)..	5 43	8 59	16 53	20 33	Reboursin (halte)..	5 2	9 26	16 6	20 52
3 »	2 30	34	Graçay.......arr. dép.	5 54 5 56	9 11 9 14	17 4 17 7	20 44 20 58	Vatan...........	5 16 5 30	9 41 10 »	16 21 16 40	21 6 ...
3 15	2 40	36	Vilaine-Coulon (h.)	6 7	9 17	17 17	...	Meunet-sr-Vatan(h)	5 42	10 12	16 52	...
3 35	2 55	40	Nohant-en-Graçay.	6 21	9 25	17 25	...	Luçay-le-Libre (h.)	5 50	10 20	17 »	...
3 75	2 85	43	Provenchères (h.).	6 31	9 41	17 41	21 29	Giroux-Villeneuve.	5 56	10 26	17 6	...
4 05	3 10	46	Massay...........	6 49	9 56	17 52	21 44	Paudy............	6 8	10 39	17 19	...
4 65	3 55	53	Port-des-St-Hil. (h.)	7 »	10 14	18 10	22 »	Les Bordes........	6 15	10 51	17 41	...
4 90	3 75	56	Vierzon-Bourgneuf	7 15	10 24	18 20	22 8	Place de Vouet (h.)	6 49	11 21	18 1	...
5 »	3 80	57	●Vierzon (P.O.) arr. (73, 90, 104)	7 22	10 35	18 32	22 22	●Issoudun (P.O.)	6 53	11 25	18 5	...

CHAPTER 5

Le PETIT ANJOU   St JEAN de LINARES TO BEAUPREAU

Centred on Angers, this meter gauge system was the CdF d'Anjou but everyone knew it as 'le Petit Anjou'. This line was built in three sections which finally connected the northern and southern parts of the system.

From Beaupreau in the south a line was first opened to Chalonnes in 1899; this was extended in 1900 to La Poissonniere where a bridge crossed the Loire. The final section to the junction station at St Jean de Linares wasn't opened until 1910, giving access to Angers.

The system faced the usual problems in the 1930's and was supposed to close down in 1939 but the advent of war reprieved it….however it couldn't last and all traffic ended in 1947 and 1948 and the system was dismantled.

Rather than dwell on that though, the postcards take us back to the early days before 1914 when the lines were indispensable to the local community.

The network was operated with a fleet of thirty 030 locomotives originally weighing 15 tons from three builders. There were twenty locomotives from Blanc Misseron, nos. 51 to 70; six from SACM numbered 21 to 26, and four from Weidknecht numbers 101 to 104. The latter were not popular with the crews for some reason.

In the 1930's two Deacauville 25 ton 130 loco were added, nos. 3809 and 3811 but they were really too heavy for the track and weren't the ideal answer to the need for more motive power. Railcars were introduced from the 1920's onwards in an effort to reduce costs but they were unable to save the railway.

The line to be described began at the junction station of Beaupreau on the line between Nantes and Cholet from where it ran north east towards Angers. The station in order were Le Pin en Mauges, St Quentin en Mauges, Bourneuf en Mauges, St Lauvent de la Plaine, Chalonnes, La Possonniere, St Martin du Fouilloux and the junction at St Jean de Linares. However, pictures of the station have been incredibly hard to find so coverage is pretty much confined to Beaupreau and Chalonnes.

One of the SACM 030 tank loco's; they were all lettered 'ANJOU' on the side tanks and buffer beams.

Beaupreau was am important junction and the facilities were quite extensive. The station was on the line from Nantes to Cholet and the line from Angers terminated here. The stack of briquettes on the left is a work of art!

The goods shed attached to the station building isn't large, suggesting that the station was more important as an interchange point than for the local traffic it generated. This is a 1920's picture.

20. - BEAUPREAU (M.-et-L.). - La Gare

There is a large four road loco shed on the left although the main depot for the system was at Angers.

The other end of the station building is seen here in this Edwardian scene, with two trains connecting in the station. On the left is a mixed train for the line this chapter will describe, to Angers, and on the right a passenger train for Nantes.

589. - BEAUPRÉAU (M. et-L.). - La Gare

261. BEAUPRÉAU (M.-et-L.)
L'Evre et le pont du chemin de fer

Lib. Deschamps, Beaupréau

260. - Beaupréau (M.-et-L.)
L'Evre près du Champ de Courses

Imp. Freulon, Beaupréau

I have only been able to find two postcards of the small intermediate stations on the line; the quality isn't great but as they are all I have they will have to suffice.

They do give the overall layout of a loop with a small station building with attached goods shed and loading platform; presumably the other stations followed the same pattern.

This is the station at Chalonnes and happily there are more pictures of this one including his attractive scene around 1910. There is a loop siding running behind the buildings and some wagons can just be made out standing on it to the left of the goods shed.

The wider view below gives more detail; there are four loops including the one behind the buildings. This was the largest town on the route so the facilities are a little more generous. Note the stop block across the rail in the foreground.

Rarely can Chalonnes station have seen such a distinguished train load of passengers! It looks as though a special train has been provided for the occasion.

The group of congressmen seem to be visiting the suspension bridge at Chalonnes; this was built by the Seguin brothers and opened in 1841.

The bridge was destroyed in the Second World war and the replacement opened in 1948.

The postcards look to date from around 1910 and the reason for the visit has eluded me….possibly a new bridge was being considered then and the First World War prevented it being built.

CHALONNES (M.-et-L.) - La gare de l'Anjou

Not a good picture but it does show the end of the goods shed, being put to good use as a billboard.

The lower picture shows the railway bridges over the river Layon, the nearer bridge carrying the tramway. The main line was part of the Paris Orleans Railway line between Niors and la Possonniere opened in 1865.

CHALONNES. — Pont de chemin de fer sur le Layon

CHALONNES-SUR-LOIRE - Gare-État

Yve Gandon, Bazar, Chalonnes

The attractive PO station, still very much unchanged today.

(...-et-L.) - La gare du chemin de fer d'Orléans

26 LA POSSONNIÈRE (M.-et-L.) Le Grand Pont de Lalleu sur la Loire

This bridge across the Loire was built in 1863 for the new PO line between Tours & St Nazaire; as it was the only way of crossing the river the tramway rails were laid between the rails of one of the standard gauge tracks. The Petit Anjou had good relations with the PO and the Etat railways and shared their facilities at several locations.

413. - LA POSSONNIÈ

LA POSSONNIÈRE (M.-et-L.). - La Gare

The Paris Orleans Railway station at La Possonniere. The tramway passed by the station but from a triangular junction a branch from it ran alongside the PO line and the tramway trains ran into the station and then reversed. The PO railway was very accommodating to the tramway and allowed the use of their station here and elsewhere. Unfortunately none of the photo's show the narrow gauge tracks.

The station is still open though the line has been singled and the part to Niort is closed.

De la Possonnière
Recevez mon meilleur Souvenir

La Possonnerie station, probably in the 1950's.

LA POSSONNIÈRE (M.-et-L.) — La Gare — L.V. phot.

This is the station at La Roche Saint Jean de Linieres where the route we have followed from Beaupreau joined the line from Cande to complete the journey into Angers.

Finally, a picture on the line showing a ballast train about to be unloaded, a labour intensive activity.

CHAQPTER6

CHALON TO MERVANS

The metre gauge line was part of the CdF Saone et Loire system which opened between 1901 and 1907. The railway was bankrupt by 1924, was taken over by the Department and managed to carry on running passenger trains until 1934.

The 30km line to Mervans was opened in three parts, between St Marcel and St Martin en Bresse first on January 25th 1901, then connecting St Marcel with Chalons on November 26th 1903 and St Martin with Mervans on September 3rd 1905.

Passengers trains stopped running in 1932, buses taking over the service, but freight traffic was still healthy and trains continued until 1941, mainly carrying sugar beet and potatoes. The line was dismantled in 1945 using German prisoners of war.

The line connected with the rest of the system in Chalon, which also had an electric street tramway.

This wonderful postcard is what attracted me to the tramway in the first place; it was taken to show that incredible horse drawn carnival float during 1914, just before the ordered world these people knew came to an end with the advent of war.

On the left, purely by chance, is a glimpse of the metre gauge station.

This is the very unusual and appealing tramway station in Chalon, with Corpet Louvet 030 tank number 10 laying down a smoke screen. The line runs out of the station straight onto the bridge over the river, as the lower postcard shows; the station building can be seen towards the centre of the picture. This was just a halt for passengers, all the freight was handled at the station adjacent to the PLM station on the other side of the river which is the station seen in the first picture.

There is scaffolding on the end wall of the station building in this view, possibly in connection with the large sign which looks to be half finished.

The lower picture shows the PLM main line station at Chalon, with possibly the tramway station on the left.

45. — Chalon-sur-Saône — Rue des Eschavannes Saint-Laurent

Edition du Grand Bazar de l'Obélisque

18. CHALON-s-SAONE — Grande-Rue Saint-Laurent. La Gare du "Tacot"

C. Lemoine, édit.

CHALON-S-SAONE
51 CHALON-SUR-SAONE. — Vue panoramique sur la Gare — LL
Edit., P. O.

The PLM station on the main line between Paris & Marseilles.

CHALON-SUR-SAONE A MERVANS

De ou pour Chalon			(43, 72, 83, 125)		A lieu les jours de foire à Mervans.				A lieu les jours de foire à Mervans.	
			●Chalon-s-Saône dép.	4 30		8 5	12 50	16 48		18 4
• 30	• 20	3	Chalon (octroi) (arr	4 32		8 7	12 52	16 50		18 6
• 30	• 20	3	Ez-Chavannes(arr f.)	4 34		8 9	12 54	16 52		18 8
• 30	• 20	3	St-Marcel(pl.)(arr f.)	4 39		8 14	12 59	16 57		18 13
• 30	• 20	3	●St-Marcel (93)	4 47		8 22	13 10	17 •		18 21
• 30	• 20	3	St-Marcel-la-N (arr f.	4 50		8 25	13 13			18 24
• 60	• 35	6	Chatenoy (arrêt f.).	4 53		8 28	13 16			18 27
• 95	• 55	9	Prondevaux (arr f.)	4 56		8 31	13 19			18 30
1 05	• 60	10	Allériot	5 •		8 35	13 23			18 34
1 15	• 70	11	Bey (halte)	5 6		8 41	13 29			18 40
1 45	• 85	14	Damerey..........	5 12		8 47	13 35			18 46
1 55	• 95	15	St-Maurice-en-Riv..	5 16		8 51	13 39			18 50
1 85	1 10	18	Bois-de-Bissy(arr f.)	5 20		8 55	13 43			18 54
2 15	1 30	21	St-Martin-en-Bresse.	5 31		9 6	13 54			19 5
2 25	1 35	22	Outre-Cosne (arr f.	5 35		9 10	13 58			19 9
2 45	1 50	24	Villegaudin (halte).	5 40		9 15	14 3			19 14
2 60	1 55	25	Serrigny	5 48		9 23	14 11			19 22
2 90	1 75	28	Glairans (halte)	5 56		9 31	14 19			19 30
3 10	1 85	30	●Mervans (70). arr	6 •		9 35	14 23			19 34

	A lieu les jours de foire à Mervans.				A lieu les jours de foire à Mervans.	
●Mervans..... dép.		6 15	11 9	15 10		16 •
Glairans (halte) ...		6 20	11 14	15 15		16 [illegible]
Serrigny..........		6 27	11 21	15 22		16 12
Villegaudin (halte)		6 31	11 25	15 26		16 16
Outre-Cosne (arr f.		6 34	11 28	15 29		16 19
St-Martin-en-Bresse		6 41	11 35	15 36		16 26
Bois-de-Bissy arr f.		6 47	11 41	15 42		16 32
St-Maurice-en-Riv.		6 52	11 46	15 47		16 37
Damerey..........		6 56	11 50	15 51		16 41
Bey (halte)........		7 2	11 56	15 57		16 47
Allériot		7 6	12 •	16 1		16 51
Prondevaux (arr f..		7 9	12 3	16 4		16 54
Chatenoy (arrêt f.).		7 12	12 6	16 7		16 57
St-Marcel-la-N.(a.f.		7 15	12 9	16 10		17 •
●St-Marcel	4 1	7 31	12 20	16 26		17 16
St-Marcel (pl.)(arr f.	4 4	7 34	12 23	16 29		17 19
Ez-Chavannes (ar f.)	4 9	7 39	12 28	16 34		17 24
Chalon (octroi) arr	4 11	7 41	12 33	16 39		17 29
●Chalon-s-Saône arr.	4 15	7 45	12 34	16 40		17 30

Three of the intermediate stations on the line, Alleriot, Damerey and Saint-Marcel showing the typical architecture used for the stations.

A surprising number of the station buildings still exist as here at Saint-Marcel.

St Martin en Bresse station with what seems to be a wooden locomotive shed on the right in the bottom picture; it seems a very odd place to have had such a facility so it may have had some other purpose. The goods shed is larger here, but the overall pattern of the station is the same.

An aerial view of the station at St Martin, seen on the right where the road curves.

Below is another wayside station, St Maurice en Riviere.

The main loco sheds were at St Marcel les Chalon, as the large piles of Briquettes indicate; sadly they were behind the photographer but the station can be seen on the right.

This is the nearest I have come to a picture of Merlans station.

The following views are of the PLM station in the town by which the tramway terminated; the line was Dijon to Saint Amour and the station is still open.

The SL Tramway terminated at a station to the left of this view sadly I cannot find any pictures of it. There were three loops and the line ended at a single tracked loco shed with a turntable in front.

MERVANS - La Gare.

It is remarkable how little changed the station is.

The tramway station was beyond the left hand platform where there was a large wooden goods transfer shed.

MERVANS - La Gare.

CHAPTER 7

THE PONTCHARRA TO ALLEVARD LES BAINS TRAMWAY.

This metre gauge tramway opened in 1895, crossing the border between Isere and Savoie. It ran from the PLM station at Pontcharra to La Rochette with a slightly later branch to Allevard les Bains leaving the main route at Detrier and following the valley of the River Breda. The route followed the road all the way so it was a classic roadside tramway. The locomotive sheds were in La Rochette.

The line closed to passengers in 1932 but goods traffic continued until 1947. Even more remarkably, the line between Pontcharra and La Rochette was then converted to standard gauge and operated until 1988.

There were five locomotives, all Buffaud et Robatel 030 Bicabines. Nos. 1 to 4 were built in 1895 to be followed by No. 5 in 1910.

The company was known as the 'PLA', short for 'Pontcharra, La Rochette and Allevard les Bains Tramway'. They'd never have fitted all that on the loco's.

However, this is the tramway that refused to die; when the freight line closed in 1988 it was taken over by a preservation group who now run tourist trains along it, so the PLA tramway lives on!

PONTCHARRA-sur-BRÉDA (Isère)
La Gare P. L. M. (extérieur) et le Tramway Pontcharra - La Rochette - Allevard-les-Bains

This is the PLM station at Pontcharra with the tramway in the forecourt and a long mixed train ready to leave.

The PLM station is on the Grenoble to Montmelian line of 1864 and is still open.

Gare de Pontcharra-sur-Breda et Tramways de La Rochette

Lib.-Edit E. Reynaud, Chambéry. - Phot Blanc. - 362

This is another view of the same location with the PLM station building on the right and the large goods shed beyond.

Apart from the station building virtually nothing has remained the same; this is the scene today.

780 PONTCHARRA. — Place de la Gare. — LL.

The PLM station building is on the left.

Detrier is where the branch to Allevard left the main route though the junction isn't apparent here. The tramway didn't go in for lavish stations!

10. LA ROCHETTE (Savoie) — Détrier - La Gare

Furin. édit., La Rochette

3093. LA ROCHETTE (Savoie) — La Gare

Coll. L. Grimal - Chambéry

This is La Rochette station; sorry it's such a poor picture. The station building is in the centre and the loco sheds can be glimpsed on the right. Trains terminated here and then reversed to run back to Allevard les Bains.

The buildings can be seen in more detail below; on the right is large goods shed. Freight traffic was always more important than passengers.

590. LA ROCHETTE (Savoie) — La Gare

There is a good crowd of people waiting to board the train in this scene.

There is a track crossing the picture from left to right, with the train standing on another almost at right angles to it. Presumably it ran to a factory of some sort.

The line certainly served local industries as the card below shows.

1341. - ALLEVARD-les-BAINS. - La Gare

That's just the toilet block in the top picture of Allevard les Bains; the station building was a large impressive stone built structure.

The lower picture is difficult to reconcile with the others; I wonder if it was taken before the large stone station building was erected. The low building in the centre does seem to have a tramway sign on the roof.

624   ALLEVARD-LES-BAINS (Isère). — La Gare   ND Phot

ALLEVARD-les-BAINS (Isère) – La Gare

This view from the other direction shows what a major effort had been made to build a station that would attract tourists to this spa town. Sadly it didn't work and this section of the line closed completely in 1932. This is the best view of the rolling stock used on the tramway. The flat roofed goods shed must be a unique structure; I've never seen anything else at all similar.

670 ALLEVARD-LES-BAINS (Isère). – La Gare. – ND Phot.

This may be the line into one of the factories in Allevard as it passes through the closed gate.

20 ALLEVARD-les-BAINS — Vue générale et le glacier de Gleyzin. — LL.

This final postcard shows the beautiful but challenging terrain that the tramway served.

You may also enjoy these books;

FRENCH MINOR RAILWAYS Vol 1

FRENCH MINOR RAILWAYS Vol 2

NARROW GAUGE INSPIRATION Vol 1

NARROW GAUGE INSPIRATION Vol 2

NARROW GAUGE INSPIRATION Vol 3

THE THIZY TRAMWAY

THE THONES—ANNECY TRAMWAY

NARROW GAUGE ON THE ILE DE RE

SCRATCHBUILT BUILDINGS THE KIRTLEY WAY

MODELLING SCENERY THE KIRTLEY WAY

KIRTLEY MODEL BUILDINGS

FOR COMMISSION BUILT LAYOUTS, BUILDINGS & OTHER STRUCTURES, ACCESSORIES, BUILDING PAPERS, BACKSCENE PACKS, INTERIOR KITS & MORE………go to

www.kirtleymodels.com

ALL MAJOR CARDS ACCEPTED

**47 KESTREL ROAD   MELTON MOWBRAY
LEICS. LE13 0AY   01664 857805
kirtleymodels@ntlworld.com**

Printed in Great Britain
by Amazon.co.uk, Ltd.,
Marston Gate.